# ¡Tocamos!

### Mexican Folk Art Music Makers in English and Spanish

Cynthia Weill
Wooden sculptures from Oaxaca by
Avelino Pérez

Time to make music!

¡Es hora de tocar música!

Let's go!

¡Vamos!

**Bring the drums . . .**

**Trae los timbales...**

the guitar . . .

la guitarra...

and a trombone.

**y un trombón.**

**Bring a double bass . . .**

**Trae un contrabajo...**

the tuba . . .

la tuba...

and an accordion.

**y un acordeón.**

**Bring the maracas . . .**

Trae las maracas...

the harp . . .

**el arpa...**

**and the singers.**

y los cantantes.

Is everyone here?

¿Estamos todos aquí?

No. Someone's missing.

**No. Falta alguien.**

**Conductor, please!**

¡La directora, por favor!

**Everyone is here.
We play music!**

**Estamos todos.
¡Tocamos música!**

*Photo by George H. Kerr*

**S**undays and festival days are special in Oaxaca, Mexico, when orchestras play in the town square (el Zócalo) for delighted audiences. The musicians and instruments in these pages exemplify these music makers. The formation depicted on the last spread of the story was arranged to reflect the setup of a traditional Mexican band.

*Photo by Cynthia Weill*

Wood carving artisan Avelino Pérez loves his state's local concerts and enjoyed using his musical birds to represent these musicians and their instruments. It took him months to hand carve every single figure to help teach children about musicians and instruments in Spanish and English.

*Photo by Cynthia Weill*

*¡Tocamos!* is the fourth book photographed by Otto Piron in the Mexican Folk Art series. He has spent much of his long career taking pictures of Mexican folk artisans and their artwork as well as musicians from all over the world.

### Dedication

To Bailey, Weill, Sloane, and Rosie. I hope you will all love books as much as I love you! And to Anne Mayagoitia, missing you, dear friend, but so grateful for your kind and generous assistance over the years and the help of your wonderful Ruth!

### Thanks to

Martina Candelaria Morgado Romero, Otto Piron, Hal Kerr, Victor Sánchez, Jaime Ruiz, Casa Panchita, Victoria Weill, Nancy Mygatt, Amy Hest, Myriam Chapman, Amy Mulvihill, Tracey Talentino, and Laura Zadoff

### Photos by Otto Piron

### Cover and Book Design by Sergio A. Gómez

Cinco Puntos Press, *an imprint of* LEE & LOW BOOKS Inc.
381 Park Avenue South, New York, NY 10016, leeandlow.com

Manufactured in China at RR Donnelley    First Edition    10 9 8 7 6 5 4 3 2 1
Book production by The Kids at Our House    The text is set in Rockwell Extra Bold and Caslon Pro
ISBN 978-1-94762-781-9 (HC)    ISBN 978-1-94762-784-0 (EBK)    Cataloging-in-Publication data is on file with the Library of Congress

FSC
www.fsc.org

MIX
Paper | Supporting
responsible forestry
FSC® C144853